SPACE STATION ACADEMY

DESTINATION: EARTH

SALLY SPRAY AND
MARK RUFFLE

WAYLAND

First published in Great Britain in 2023
by Wayland

PB ISBN: 978 1 5263 2078 0

Editor: Paul Rockett
Design and illustration: Mark Ruffle
www.rufflebrothers.com

MIX
Paper from responsible sources
FSC® C104740
www.fsc.org

Manufactured, printed and assembled
in Dubai, UAE
First printing, April 2024 OP/04/24
28 27 26 25 24 1 2 3 4 5 6

Wayland
An imprint of Hachette Children's Group
Part of Hodder & Stoughton
Carmelite House
50 Victoria Embankment
London EC4Y 0DZ

A Hachette UK company
www.hachette.co.uk
www.hachettechildrens.co.uk

Picture credits:
Page 30 NASA/Robert and Marit Jentoft-Nilsen, based on MODIS data/JPL; page 31 NASA/JSC

SAFETY PRECAUTIONS

We recommend adult supervision at all times while doing the experiments in this book. Always be aware that ingredients may contain allergens, so check the packaging for allergens if there is a risk of an allergic reaction. Anyone with a known allergy must avoid these.

- Wear an apron and cover surfaces.
- Tie back long hair.
- Ask an adult for help with cutting.
- Check all ingredients for allergens.
- Clear up all spills right away.

Welcome to Space Station Academy, the amazing interstellar school that travels through space. Come on board and learn about our solar system.

Contents

Meet the team

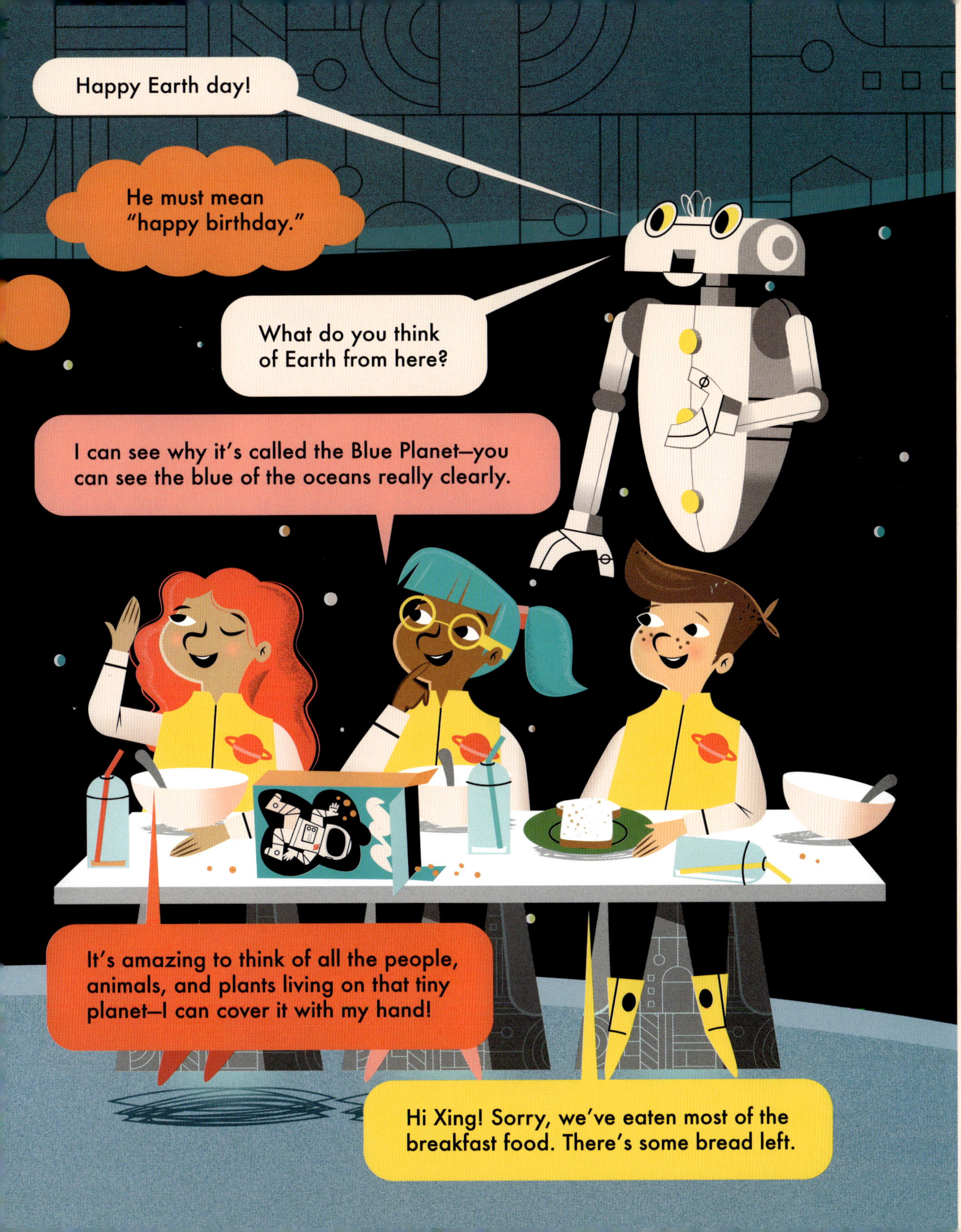
Happy Earth day!
He must mean "happy birthday."
What do you think of Earth from here?
I can see why it's called the Blue Planet—you can see the blue of the oceans really clearly.
It's amazing to think of all the people, animals, and plants living on that tiny planet—I can cover it with my hand!
Hi Xing! Sorry, we've eaten most of the breakfast food. There's some bread left.

In the classroom...
Today we're visiting Earth! There's a lot to see and learn about. What do you know already?
It's the third planet from the Sun. It's a terrestrial planet, which means it has a rocky surface like Mercury, Venus, and Mars.
It's the fifth largest planet in the solar system. It has a diameter of 7,950 miles.

It has one moon that orbits Earth every 28 days.
I'm so sad.
Your turn, Xing. Xing? Are you okay?
They remember all these things about Earth, but they haven't remembered my birthday.

Earth came into existence about 4.5 billions years ago. It formed from a swirling cloud of dust and gas orbiting the Sun.

1

Hot liquid rock, called magma, cooled to form rocky land on the surface.

The magma caused steam to form clouds. Rain from the clouds helped create the oceans, along with ice from comets that landed on Earth.

4

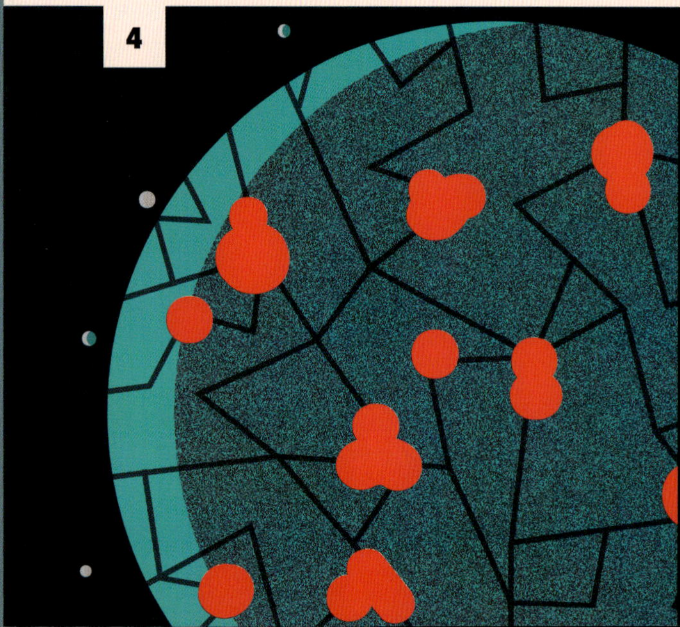

5

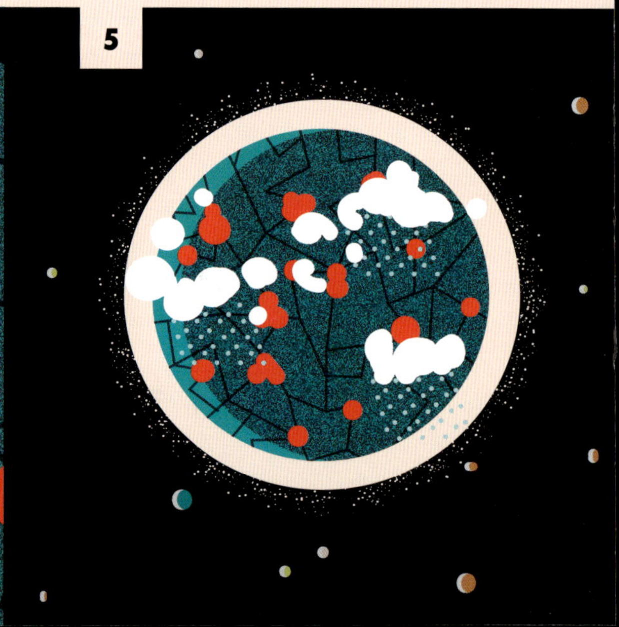

Gravity made the dust and rocks clump together until they formed one huge, hot, spinning ball.

As the young planet spun around, layers formed inside and its outside cooled to form a delicate crust.

2

3

Around 300 million years ago, Earth had one large land mass called Pangea and one ocean called Panthalassa.

The land was made from overlapping tectonic plates that split and moved to form the continents and oceans we see today.

6

7

It's a special day today.
It certainly is!
We can go for a space walk outside to take a closer look at Earth.
Oh!
Outside the Academy...
This is an amazing view! What's that pale blue border around Earth?
That's Earth's atmosphere. It's a layer of gases held in place by gravity.
It's like a big birthday balloon wrapped around Earth!

The atmosphere contains the gas oxygen, which humans and animals need to breathe.
The atmosphere traps heat from the Sun, which keeps Earth warm and stops it from getting too hot or too cold.
Psst ... Dr. Bott! Can we let Xing know we've remembered his birthday?

Earth is amazing inside and out!
The inside of Earth is called the geosphere. It has four layers.
The crust is 3 to 43 miles thick and made of rock and minerals. It's the part we stand on!
The mantle is hot and made of solid rock and squishy magma.
The outer core is made from liquid iron and nickel.
The inner core is made from solid iron and nickel. Intense pressure keeps the metals solid.
It's funny to think of all those layers under your feet on Earth!

Earth is interesting, but why have they forgotten my birthday?
Poor Xing. He's gone back to the Academy. He thinks we've forgotten.
Get the banner out, kids!
Xing!
HAPPY BIRTHDAY XING!

Later...
Call out to let me know you're ready to go.
Have fun on Earth—see you later!
Present!
Present!
Present!
Not one birthday present.

Earth orbits the Sun in 365 days, 5 hours, 59 minutes, and 16 seconds. This is a year.

And we ALL have one birthday a year!

Wow! What a great view of Earth spinning and going around the Sun.

A day is 24 hours long, the time it takes Earth to spin around once.

Look at the sunlight shining on this side of the Earth!

Earth spins around an axis. For those places on Earth that are facing the Sun, it's daytime. When they spin away from the Sun, it's nighttime.

What is an axis?

An axis is like an invisible stick that goes through the planet's North and South Poles. The Earth's axis is tilted at 23.5 degrees. This is why there are seasons.

The Earth rotates on its axis at the same time as it orbits the Sun. The axis always points in the same direction.

For half the year, the top of the planet, the Northern Hemisphere, is angled toward the Sun and has longer, hotter days. Meanwhile, the bottom of the planet, the Southern Hemisphere, has shorter, colder days.

Let's take a fly-by and see for ourselves. When it's summer in Sydney in Australia, in the Southern Hemisphere ...
it's winter in New York, USA, in the Northern Hemisphere. Let's make our first stop on Earth and learn some more.

First stop: the Amazon Rainforest.

Why is Earth the only planet with life, Dr. Bott?

It has to do with Earth's position in the solar system.

It's in just the right place to be not too hot and not too cold. It's just right for life to exist. This position is called the Goldilocks or habitable zone.

Our neighbor, Venus, is too hot and Mars is too cold.

Back to the pod! Lots more to see and do!

This *is* a pretty exciting birthday trip!

Next stops: amazing natural landmarks!

Although Earth is unique, it does share many features with the other terrestrial planets and moons.

Look! A volcano!

Yes, Melody—this is Mauna Loa in Hawaii. It's the largest volcano on Earth. It's 2.5 miles above sea level, and 3.1 miles below sea level. It's tiny compared to Olympus Mons on Mars, which is 15.5 miles high. Volcanoes have helped to shape the landscape on all the rocky planets.

And here we are on Mount Everest. This is the tallest mountain on Earth at 29,032 feet high.

The tallest in the solar system is Rheasilvia on the asteroid Vesta, at 13.7 miles high!

It's windy! I hope we don't get blown off—it's a long way to fall!

Here's Niagara Falls! This magnificent waterfall is between Canada and the USA. The water falls 167 feet down to the river below. It's not as big as the Echus Chasma waterfalls that were on Mars. Water there poured over a 13,000-foot drop.

This is the Barringer Meteor Crater in the Arizona Desert. It's one of over 170 crater sites on Earth. It was made about 50,000 years ago by an iron meteorite. Our moon has over 100,000 craters including the largest in the solar system, South Pole-Aitken basin!

Now to show you the hottest and coldest places on Earth.

Can you see the two snowy patches at the top and bottom of Earth? In the center of these are the North and South Poles, the coldest places on Earth.

It is hottest in the middle of the planet along an invisible line called the Equator. This area is always closest to the Sun.

Xing, where would you like to go?
A cold Pole place or a hot Equator place?

Hmm, cold please!

Brrrr! It is cold! Where are we?
The snow's so pretty, like icing on a birthday cake!
We're near the North Pole. There's no land here, just 10-foot-thick ice.
Does anything live here?
Yes! Polar bears live here and hunt seals. Arctic foxes live here too and hunt Arctic hares. There are also narwhals and orcas that hunt for fish.
The frozen sea ice is important. It's so white, it helps to reflect heat back into space and keep Earth cool.

Next stop: underwater.

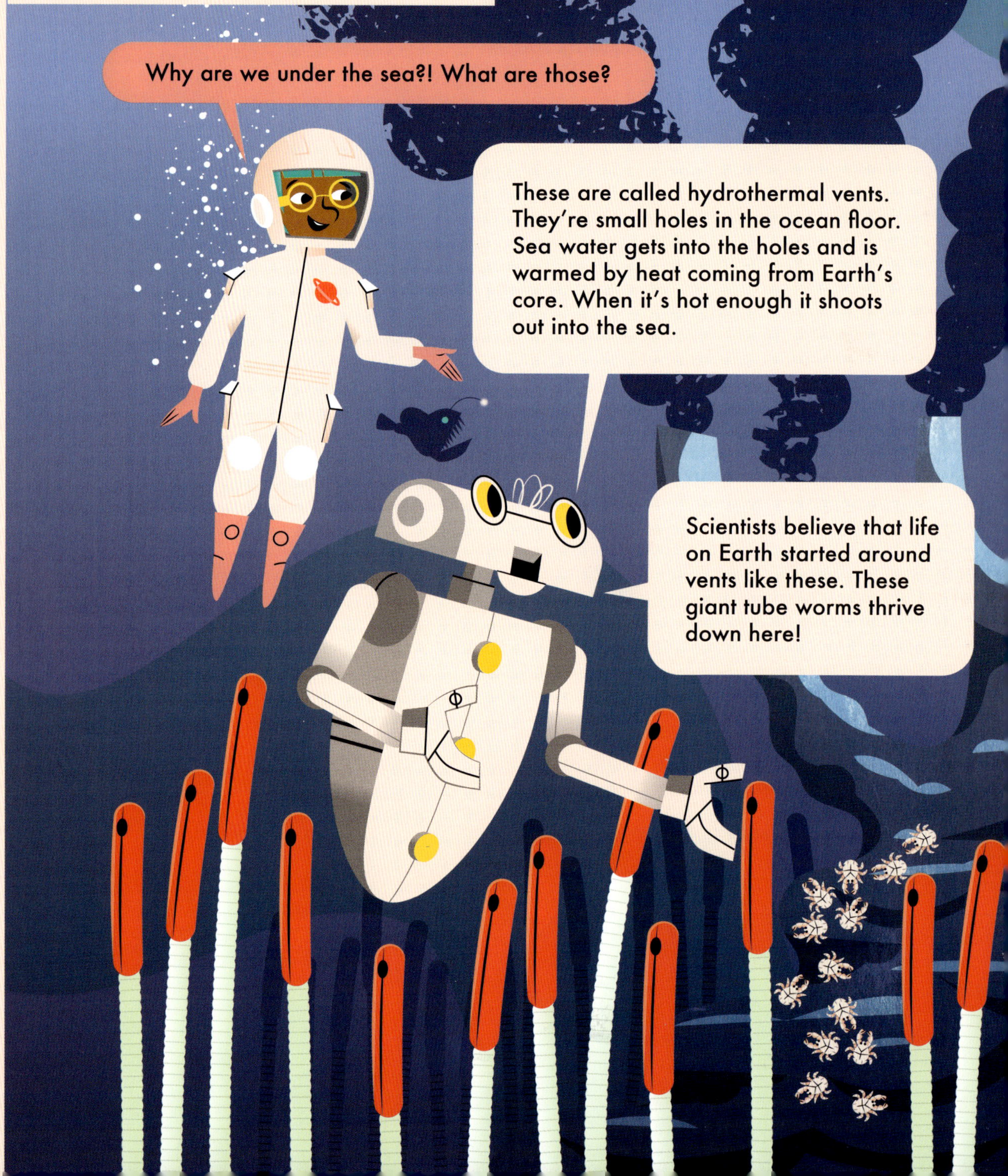

They look amazing! A bit like giant birthday candles!
Hmph!
Those crabs look like they're having a party! Shall we have one too, Dr. Bott? We've kept Xing waiting long enough. Let's head back up to dry land.

Final stop: Xing's birthday party!

Hello, Botty!
HAPPY BIRTHDAY XING!
Happy birthday, Xing!
Xing, we've been giving you clues all day!
What a great party!

Space Academy Activities

The Space Academy gang have been so inspired by their mission to Earth, they wanted to find out more. Will you join them?

Dr. Bott's Space Experiment

Earth is lit by light coming from the Sun. Light travels in a straight line, so if an object blocks the light, it casts a shadow. Let's use a shadow to make a clock!

Equipment

- A sunny day
- A stick or a pencil stuck in modeling clay
- Paper or stones
- A pen

Method

Place your stick in the ground, or your pencil in the modeling clay on a piece of paper. Make sure there is space around the stick for a shadow to fall.

Draw a mark at the end of the shadow or place a stone at that point. Mark the time on the stone or the paper.

Check back each hour and record where the shadow is.

You've made a shadow clock; humans have been making these for over 5,000 years!

Outcomes

What happens to the shadow when a cloud moves over the Sun?

What happens to the shadow during the day?

Don't move your clock, then test it the next day to see if the times recorded still match up.

Another Sunlight Experiment

Write a secret message for a friend (maybe a birthday greeting) using lemon juice instead of ink. Leave the message in sunlight and watch the words magically appear!

Melody's Earth Fact

71 percent of Earth's surface is covered with water.

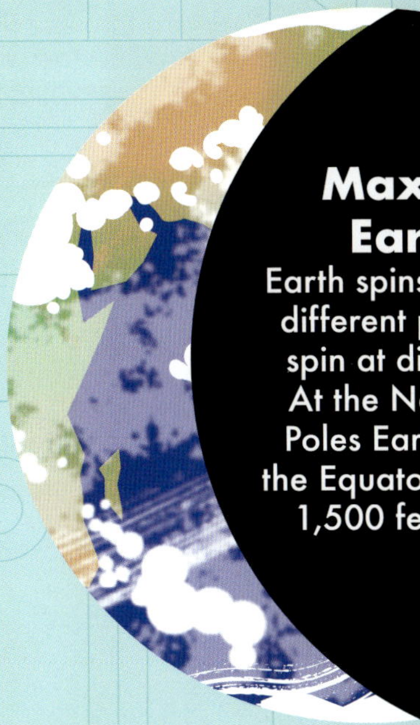

Max's Extra Earth Fact

Earth spins really fast, and different places on Earth spin at different speeds. At the North and South Poles Earth is still, but at the Equator it's traveling at 1,500 feet per second.

Xing's Earth Math Problem

The circumference of Earth is 24,900 miles. If you traveled in a straight line around the world at 15 mph, how many days would it take you? Round your answer up to the nearest day. And for extra fun, find out how many countries the Equator passes through—what's special about this number?

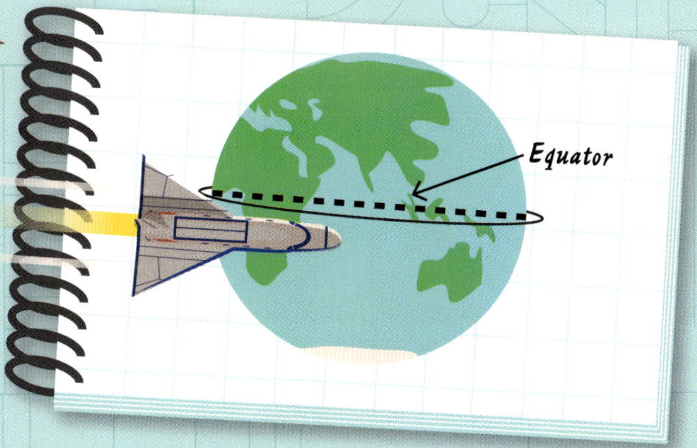

Answer: 70 days. 13 countries—it's a prime number.

Stella's Earth Picture Gallery

This is Earth. Look how much of it is covered with water, clouds, and ice. Can you see any land?

The Earth and the Moon, clearly showing day and night. Where was the Sun when this was taken?

Mo's Research Project

Find out about meteorite craters on Earth. Where are they? How big are they? Then compare them to craters found on other planets.

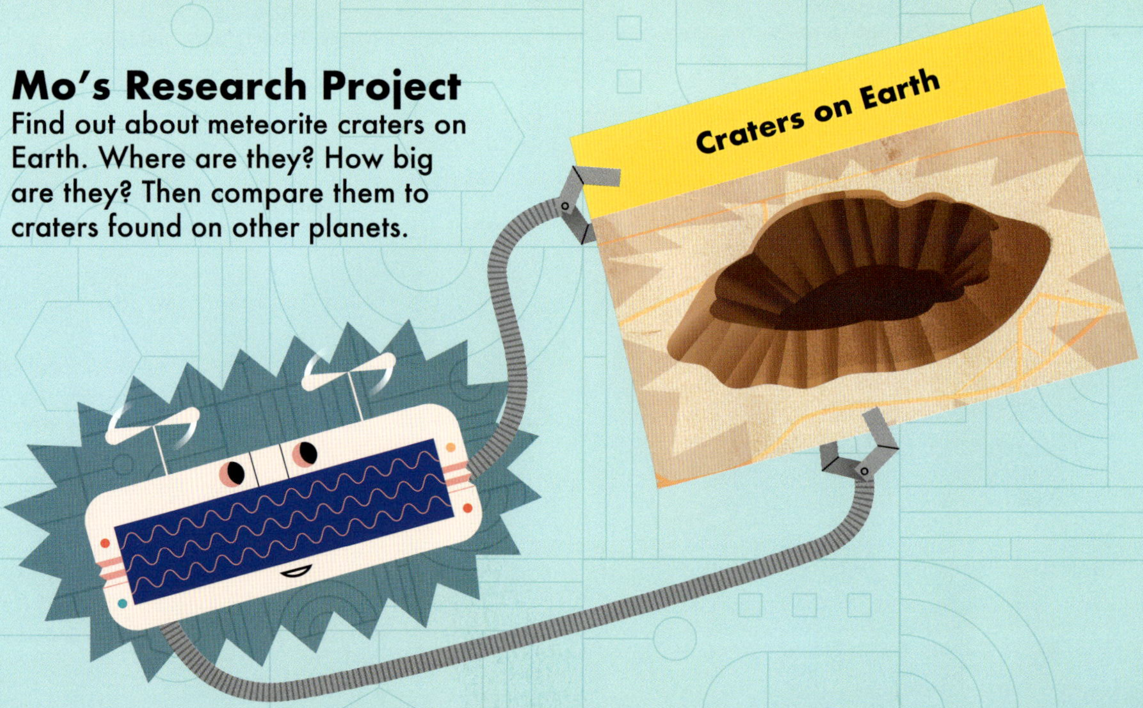

In the atmosphere above Canada, we can see the Aurora Borealis spreading across the sky. What is this? Can you see the lights on the ground below?

Look! A swirling whirling hurricane over the Pacific Ocean.

Further information

Wonderful websites

rainforest-alliance.org/resource/kids
natgeokids.com/uk/discover/science/space/facts-about-the-earth
spaceplace.nasa.gov/menu/earth
kids.britannica.com/kids/article/Earth/353074

Awesome books

Dr. Maggie's Grand Tour of the Solar System by Dr. Maggie Aderin-Pocock (Buster Books, 2019)
So Many Questions About Space by Sally Spray (Wayland, 2022)
Wonders of the Night Sky by Professor Raman Prinja (Wayland, 2022)

Glossary

asteroid—a small rocky object that orbits the Sun
atmosphere—the layer of gas surrounding a planet
axis—the imaginary line around which an object, such as a planet, rotates
circumference—the measurement around the edge of a circle
comet—a lump of ice, dust, and rock that orbits the Sun
core—the center of something, such as a planet
crater—a large, bowl-shaped hole in the surface of something, such as a moon
crust—the outer or top layer of a planet
diameter—the measurement across the middle of a sphere or circle
gravity—the force of attraction that pulls one thing toward another
interstellar—describes something that is located or happens between stars
meteorite—a space rock that has fallen through a planet's atmosphere and landed on its surface
minerals—solid substances made of chemicals that form naturally on Earth, such as quartz and sulfur
moon—a natural body that orbits a planet
orbit—to travel around a star or planet
pressure—the amount of push force on something
solar system—the Sun and the objects in orbit around it
tectonic plates—massive, moving pieces of rock that make up Earth's crust

Index